25 Quick Mini-Lessons to Teach
Narrative Writing

By Dave Leochko

SCHOLASTIC
PROFESSIONAL BOOKS

New York • Toronto • London • Auckland • Sydney
Mexico City • New Delhi • Hong Kong

Dedication

For Cole and Teal

Acknowledgments

I would like to thank Myron, Sharon, and Barry—my teaching colleagues and friends.

Cover design by Mo Bing Chan
Cover illustration by Eric Brace
Interior design by Drew Hires
Interior illustrations by Drew Hires

ISBN 0-439-06396-5

Table of Contents

Introduction

*D*eveloping an effective writing program is a long process for a teacher. Not only do teachers have to become familiar with the writing process, but they also need to find lessons that are appropriate for their students. When I first started teaching writing, I found many professional books that discussed teaching the writing process, including suggestions for getting students to conference with other students and revise and edit their own work. What I couldn't find was reproducible materials that would help me teach students about these parts of the writing process.

I decided that I would put together my own reproducible lessons. It took me a great deal thought and time, but in the end I had a packet of materials I could always refer to. These lessons have become valuable tools for helping me demonstrate the writing process.

The origin of this book was a discussion between my principal and myself about professional materials for teachers. Many professional books focus on teaching philosophies and methodologies. They provide teachers with the teaching rationale. But, while understanding the philosophy is important, this does not make the classroom run. Daily lessons and activities do that. They help us put our philosophy into action. Developing lessons and activities, as all teachers know, takes an incredible amount of time, so it is essential for teachers to have sources to turn to for lessons.

Many teachers fall under the misconception that all lessons must be first-hand, fresh ideas in order for them to be meaningful. Teachers do not need to reinvent the wheel each time a lesson is presented. A good teacher is a collector of lessons. He or she looks at everything as a source of ideas. Reproducible activities are just one more source for teachers. Teachers can turn to such activities and modify them to fit their students' needs.

In this book, you will find lessons that have been successful for me. You may find they work just right for you, or you can adapt them to suit your needs. In any event I have compiled them here for you to have at your fingertips. They are meant to help you cut down on preparation time so that you can enjoy being actively involved in teaching the writing process.

Part One

Getting Started

Writing process has been given much attention lately, but many people—especially parents—wonder how this style of writing is different from the writing students have always done in school. It is part of our job as teachers to help parents sift through the jargon to understand what it is their children are engaged in.

Traditionally in schools, teachers and students paid attention to only two parts of the writing process—initiating an idea and the final version of that idea. Students were assigned or selected a topic and on the due date they handed in a piece of polished work. How to get to that final product was not taught, but the final product was, of course, read and evaluated.

Teaching the writing process involves the two familiar points as well as guiding students through all the other "stuff" that comes in between that initial idea and the end result. It is a system in which all the stages of writing are valued, not just the finished product. All that "messy stuff" of fixing up stories is brought out in the classroom, and given as much prominence as the final product that is posted on the bulletin board.

Many of us have been engaged in the writing process quite naturally. In college, when we were required to write an essay, we may have written down our ideas, consulted a friend as a sounding board, sought a few opinions, and then proceeded to fix up our paper. We would correct it because we knew our professors would not accept a story or essay that didn't make sense or had spelling mistakes. Then we probably rewrote or retyped the piece to make it look presentable enough for others to read. Of course, we still knew that the most important part of the process was the final copy.

Creating Mini-Lessons for Teaching Writing

Most people learn the process of writing by doing. A writer needs to be engaged in revision to have a true understanding of it. A writer learns to edit by sitting down and editing. This is the best way to teach students how to write. However, there are some fundamental principles behind the process, and that is what the mini-lessons should focus on.

Initially, I was presenting these principles through discussion but I soon discovered that students were quickly forgetting the ideas. If I was using the overhead projector or chalkboard to introduce a concept and to demonstrate a process, once the example was erased it was often erased from the students' consciousness. I realized that presenting the concept was just not enough; students had to experience the process as well.

It was then that I decided to introduce writing handbooks into my lessons. I gave each student a two-pocket folder they could fill with the mini-lesson handouts. I told them that over the course of the year, they would compile a handbook that contained valuable information on writing. This handbook would be something they could refer to during writing workshops and even keep as a reference for the future.

Then I began to develop reproducible sheets on the stages of the writing process. Some contain short activities that we take up within the period and others contain specific information that become the basis for discussion.

Many of the mini-lessons and activities in this book are reproducibles created for students' writing handbooks. Some can be used to introduce a concept. They can be copied onto an overhead transparency and shared with the class, and copies can be given to students so they can refer to them when needed. Other mini-lessons include reproducible practice sheets that help students apply the skills immediately.

Introducing the Writing Steps

I use an eight-step approach to writing. At the beginning of the year, I introduce these steps to students and give them each a copy of The Writing Steps (page 15). I also create posters that list the steps to hang in the classroom. Then the class is ready to embark on our writing journey.

Through years of trial and error, I discovered that mini-lessons had to follow one another in some kind of pattern that included times for practice. Inundating students with a new mini-lesson each day was too overwhelming. It did not give them enough time to familiarize themselves with the lessons or internalize the process introduced. I found that teaching a mini-lesson every second or third day was the most comfortable pace for all of us.

The pace of the mini-lessons is just one of many things that I have refined, rethought, and revised over the years of teaching writing. The following section is a collection of thoughts about each of the steps in process writing.

Steps 1 & 2: Getting an Idea and Writing a Draft

Our initial writing periods start with students selecting a topic from a short list of ideas they have generated. The topics are ideas that interest them or things they know and want to write about. In these early stages of the writing process, a teacher will see which students have the ability to generate ideas. These children quickly dive into their work, writing reams of pages on a multitude of topics.

But in each classroom there are students who say they can't think of anything to write about. I have also wondered if I am limiting children in their writing when I tell them to write about their own experiences. Are all of Madeleine L'Engle's stories about things she experienced firsthand? So, to help students get started, I begin by having them look around for sources of ideas for writing. I ask them to be aware of the world around them and how anything can be a potential source for writing. In addition, I model different types of story structures and genres they can use and introduce them to other writing formats, such as a newspaper article, to show to them all the kinds of writing there are.

Step 3: Conferencing

Conferencing has always been one of the most difficult parts of the process to manage. To conference effectively, students need to learn how to give constructive criticism. Students who conference with a friend are often concerned about hurting their friend's feelings when they express a criticism. Sometimes, if a student does not have a true interest in another person's writing, he might not

want to invest the energy needed to offer suggestions for improvement.

However, I find the main reason students have trouble with conferencing is that they lack the skill and knowledge necessary to examine a piece of writing. They don't yet know what to look for in a piece of writing or how to give advice. Teaching this process step is important if we wish to build a sense of community in our classrooms, and I have created mini-lessons to address this stage of the process.

Step 4: Revising

Often students want to rush through the revision process. It is probably the hardest part of the writing process. We struggle with it as a class throughout the year. Even adults are reluctant. After all it is not as exciting as creating new ideas, nor does it bring the tangible end product of the publishing stage. Revising can also make us feel our areas of weakness are being highlighted.

It is this attitude we need to overcome, and I guarantee you that it is something you will have to work on with students throughout the year. I try to get my kids to accept the idea that revising is not correcting mistakes, it is editing; changing something does not imply a mistake, but rather it is making an improvement.

I tell my students that revising is taking your great ideas and making them even better by communicating them to readers. I like to use the following analogy: Writing a rough draft it is like baking a cake. When you are done you have something quite tasty, but it is a plain cake, and while it may be good that way, there is something we can do to the cake to make it taste even better. We can put icing on it, or sprinkles, or candied roses. That is what revising is, taking something ordinary and making it extraordinary. Revision is a crucial step to establish in our classes. It is during the revision process that we teach many of the important writing skills.

Step 5: Decide the Writing Is Set

This step requires decision-making skills. If students are to become effective writers, they need to develop the skills for assessing when a work is finished. What impact does step five have on writers? Look at two different scenarios.

Some students embarking on the writing process want to publish every piece of work they produce. Not only is this time consuming but it means the student is not reflecting on his or her writing. On the other hand, there are students who would be content to spend all their time on the same piece of writing for the whole year. These students feel their writing just isn't ready yet. In being so judgmental, they do not thoroughly engage in the entire writing process.

After introducing this step, I ask students for a rationale for their decision to publish particular pieces of writing. Initially it is hard for students to articulate their thoughts, but as the year progresses they become more comfortable with constructive self-criticism, which helps them become more effective writers.

Step 6: Final Self-Editing/Peer-Editing

Students often edit their pieces on a fast track. They have put a lot of time and energy into their drafts and are anxious to engage in publishing. But editing is not only important for the students to learn, it is also extremely important with regards to classroom management. My ultimate goal in the year is to have students become skilled enough at editing that they can help themselves and others. When this starts to happen, I can focus my time on helping writers develop, as opposed to spending all my time correcting stories.

Step 7: Teacher-Editing

This step is one of the few of the process for which I do not provide handouts. It's more procedure than process for students. I explain to students that once they have completed their editing and have had another student peer-edit their work, it is time for a teacher edit. I have students deposit their stories in a box labeled Stories to Be Edited. I have quickly learned not to make promises about when I would return their pieces. I explain that they outnumber me, and they have to be patient about getting their stories back. In the meantime, they may do some preparations for the publishing stage or go back to step one and work on another piece.

I do the editing in many different ways. If I notice a student having problems with a specific area, I may have her sit with me, and we'll edit the story together. (Often this is done during the writing workshop period since the level of independence among writers grows quickly.) If I see a student writing with few problems, I may edit his work at another time to speed things up. I may return the story with a brief note or have a quick five-minute discussion about the story. The next time I edit that student's work, we'll conference more extensively.

Occasionally, I will ask an outside person, such as a resource teacher, teacher's assistant, student teacher, or volunteer, to do some editing with a student. This also gives me a different perspective on the student and the student a new view of her writing.

As I edit a student's work, I pull out a recording sheet that I keep on the child and jot down a few observations on writing style and skill. I may include such information as knowledge of character, setting, spelling, and grammar. This is an important source of record keeping and assessment.

Step 8: Publishing

I refer to publishing as a time to go public, a time to share our ideas with everybody. Publishing is important because it develops the sense of community among the learners. It also validates the importance of the writing process. There is an end result to our work—it is to share our thoughts with others. If children understand there is a reason for the process, then they will be more willing to engage in it.

Managing Writing in the Classroom

Mini-Lesson 1 Your Job as a Writer

Children are most comfortable when they know the parameters that exist for them. When I first began to teach writing, I did not want to put too many demands on my students. I wanted them to keep their attention and focus on their writing. I soon discovered that I often had to interrupt valuable classroom time to explain what was expected of a writer. Rather than stopping the class each and every time to discuss an expectation, I created a reproducible handout that gave students overall guidelines for the writing program.

I use this reproducible, Your Job as a Writer (page 16), as the basis for the first writing mini-lesson of the year. I hand out copies of the guidelines and also create a poster that lists the guidelines to post in the classroom. Setting standards lets students clearly know what is expected and also provides a sense of fairness: students know that the rules will not change without warning and that they are the same for everybody. Even though everyone will not be able to meet all these expectations initially, the guidelines are goals that students can work

Your Job as a Writer

1. Come to class every day with your writing folder, in which you'll keep all the drafts of your writing.

2. Take care of your writing folder.

3. Write every day and finish pieces of writing.

4. Make plans for your writing and wo on it both during class and at home

5. Always look for writing topics that care about.

6. Take risks as a writer: try new top techniques, and new types of writ

7. Write using paragraphs.

8. Work on editing your final drafts

9. Make final copies legible and co

10. Take care of the writing material used in class.

16

Putting Together a Collector's Folder

Writers are always looking for ideas, and they can find them everywhere they look. Ideas can come from an interesting newspaper article, an overheard conversation, or an intriguing photograph.

Spend some time being a collector. Here's how:

✔ Cut out stories in newspapers and magazines that look interesting to you.
✔ Write down any interesting lines or pieces of dialogue that you hear.
✔ Jot down the main idea of a dream.
✔ Cut out photos of favorite people, places, and things from calendars, brochures, and so on.
✔ Collect photos of friends or people you have met (or wish to meet).
✔ Start a list of names of people and places that you like.
✔ Collect pictures of exciting scenes or ones that make you think.
✔ Make a list of "I wonder..." questions.

Put all the materials you collect in a folder and keep it beside you when you write. You'll be able to pull ideas from your folder whenever you need to. Remember to keep collecting material. Pretty soon you'll never be without a writing idea.

18

towards. I have discovered that students rise to the expectations provided to them.

My guidelines have come from my personal reading on the topic of writing as well as my personal experiences. You might need to adapt and adjust guidelines to fit the needs of your classroom.

Another tool I use to foster responsibility is My Writing Planner (page 17), a reproducible outline that students can use to plan what writing they will work on each week. It helps students learn how to plan, organize, and then carry out their goals.

Mini-Lesson 2 Collector's Folder

I start this mini-lesson by explaining to students that when a writer sits down to plan out a story, he or she has already done a lot of work before writing even one word. I explain to them that writers are always looking at the world around them for story ideas. Stories can be found everywhere, including in news stories, conversations, photographs, dreams, and so on. Sometimes the start of a story can be an "I wonder. . ." question. Stories also start from personal experiences. They may be events that happened to the author or other people the author may know.

During this discussion, I share with students my "collector's folder." Students are always fascinated with this: they feel it gives them a peek into their teacher's head. I explain how my collector's folder is a place where I keep all my ideas for writing. Whenever I read or hear something interesting, I add it to my folder for future use. My folder contains pictures from magazines, newspaper clippings, post-it notes of words, phrases I have overheard, and so on.

After spending time going through my folder and telling students about the origins of some of the material, I explain to students that they will spend the next week creating their own collector's folder. I distribute a copy of Putting Together a Collector's Folder (page 18) and provide each student with a two-pocket folder. After a week, we have a sharing session in which students talk about the material they have collected. I often have students share their folders with a partner or in small groups.

The Idea Bank

As a follow-up, I ask students to donate ideas for a bulletin board we call the Idea Bank. I post the ideas on the bulletin board, updating the bank throughout the year. I tell students that in the future, if they don't have an idea, they should browse through their collector's folder or borrow an idea from the Idea Bank. We continually update our folders and also have swap days on which we trade ideas from each other's folders. In this way, students are always on the lookout for good topics and can draw from an ever-expanding pool of ideas.

The Idea Box

After spending the first month of school establishing the writing process and getting students started writing stories, I like to add other components to my writing workshops. In the second month of school, I introduce the Idea Box. Inside the Idea Box are file folders that feature different ideas and formats for writing. Each folder is labeled with a specific writing form, such as rebus story, advice column, or song. Mounted on the outside of the folder is a brief definition of that writing form, and inside the folder are samples of the writing form.

Once a week, I gather the class and present a new writing form from the Idea Box. I explain the writing form, share samples with the class, and discuss the characteristics of the form. Sometimes I use overhead transparencies to share examples with the class. These presentations are simply to show students other options for writing. I don't immediately ask students to use the format for a writing assignment. Instead, when I find students struggling to find a writing idea, I suggest they visit the Idea Box for some inspiration.

I usually find that when one student attempts a new format, others will then follow. For example, once a student writes a quiz, publishes it, and either presents it at sharing time or posts the sample on the bulletin board, then other students are more willing to take a risk and try the new form.

Topics in the Idea Box are usually shorter forms and so provide students with

a refreshing break from longer narrative writing assignments. These options also allow students who are struggling with traditional forms to experience success and find strengths they were unaware of. Also, students see the many different types of writing that exist. Even with these projects, students still follow all of the writing-process steps.

An Idea Box can be put together over time. I started with only five or six folders, and each year I have managed to add two or three new folders. I began by collecting samples of the different types of writing, collecting postcards and brochures, snipping-out advice columns from kid's magazines, and looking for interviews in various publications. When I have a number (for example, five or six) samples of a particular format, I create a folder for the Idea Box.

Use the Idea-Box Cards (pages 19-21) to start your own Idea Box. Each card features a brief definition of a type of writing and can be copied, cut out, and attached to a folder.

Mini-Lesson 3 Story Structure

While there is an emphasis in the writing process on encouraging students to generate their own ideas and stories, we need to introduce students to different story structures and genres. It is important not only to teach students the process of writing, but also to model the genres and structures they can use in their writing.

Creating stories modeled on traditional story structures has taken a back seat in recent years, but it is important to remind ourselves that modeling is in itself a writing skill that many professional writers use. For example, Graeme Base's *Anamalia* is a sophisticated model of a traditional alphabet book. When we read it, we marvel at the creativity involved, but when our intermediate students tell us they are going to construct an ABC book we often hesitate to accept their plan, believing there is not enough of a challenge involved. *The Book That Jack Wrote* by Jon Scieszka is another book modeled on a classic tale. Many success-ful authors have published retellings of Grimm's fairytales.

We should allow our students the same plea-sure we receive from this form of writing by let-ting them create books and stories modeled on traditional structures and genres. That is why, once students become comfortable with the writ-ing process, I begin modeling story structures.

It is important to remember that modeling story structures is a process. Simply reading a version of a story structure is not enough. We have to allow students the time to internalize the concepts. We may have children who have experiences with a story structure but are not aware of the construction used in the structure. Other students may be encountering a particular story structure for the first time.

Story-Structure Cards

To start the modeling process, I begin by reading published versions of particu-lar structures and provide students with definitions of the story structure. The reproducible Story-Structure Cards (pages 22-23) also introduce students to dif-ferent types of stories. These can be posted on a bulletin board or kept with samples of the stories.

The next step is to look for another example of the structure in question. I may present a version published by a previous student or one that I have written. (To build a collection of samples, I try to have somebody donate a copy of each type of writing that we do.) If I do not have a sample to show, we may then start a class story that uses the structure. As a class we brainstorm ideas, allowing children a chance to see how they can incorporate their ideas into the framework. Occasionally you may want to use another published book that models the structure. The presentations allow students the opportunity to apply an existing form to their own ideas.

Observing and Evaluating the Process

If I find students struggling with elements of a story structure, I first make some observation notes about their struggles, then discuss what I've seen with them. We examine which features are missing and how they can be included.

In the end, if a student's writing does not fit the existing structure, even after revision, we leave it as is. Though it may not fit the existing pattern, it is still a valuable piece of writing for the student. In my notes I include an observation along the lines of, "Has not internalized existing pattern, needs more opportunities to work with story structure."

For those students who go off to model a successful version without any difficulty, I may include a note about their ease at internalizing the structure or comment on the content. A comment might be, "Able to use parody in existing structure" or "Ability to write ficitionalized versions of real-life situations."

Mini-Lesson 4 Tall Tales

Exploring different genres can be done in conjunction with the class's reading workshop periods or in the form of a mini-lesson during writing workshop. Some of the genres that we have explored in the past include realistic fiction, science fiction, biography, fantasy, mystery, historical fiction, tall tales, fairy tales, legends, and myths.

I model genres using the same process I used to model story structures. I give students a definition of the genre, share examples with the class, and give them directions for creating their own versions of the genre. Tall Tales (page 24) is a reproducible that introduces students to this genre and is an example of how to explain a genre's key components.

Writing Steps

1. Rehearse (Find an Idea)

2. Draft One

3. Conference

4. Draft Two (Revise)

5. Decide the Writing Is Set

6. Final Self-Edit/Peer-Edit

7. Teacher-Edit

8. Final Copy—Go Public!

Your Job as a Writer

1. Come to class every day with your writing folder, in which you'll keep all the drafts of your writing.

2. Take care of your writing folder.

3. Write every day and finish pieces of writing.

4. Make plans for your writing and work on it both during class and at home.

5. Always look for writing topics that you care about.

6. Take risks as a writer: try new topics, new techniques, and new types of writing.

7. Write using paragraphs.

8. Work on editing your final drafts.

9. Make final copies legible and correct.

10. Take care of the writing materials used in class.

Name _____

My Writing Planner

	Monday	Tuesday	Wednesday	Thursday	Friday
Date:					
My Plans/ Goals					
How I Did					
Additional Comments (By Teacher/ Student)					

Putting Together a Collector's Folder

Writers are always looking for ideas, and they can find them everywhere they look. Ideas can come from an interesting newspaper article, an overheard conversation, or an intriguing photograph.

Spend some time being a collector. Here's how:

✔ Cut out stories in newspapers and magazines that look interesting to you.

✔ Write down any interesting lines or pieces of dialogue that you hear.

✔ Jot down the main idea of a dream.

✔ Cut out photos of favorite people, places, and things from calendars, brochures, and so on.

✔ Collect photos of friends or people you have met (or wish to meet).

✔ Start a list of names of people and places that you like.

✔ Collect pictures of exciting scenes or ones that make you think.

✔ Make a list of "I wonder..." questions.

Put all the materials you collect in a folder and keep it beside you when you write. You'll be able to pull ideas from your folder whenever you need to. Remember to keep collecting material. Pretty soon you'll never be without a writing idea.

How-to Instructions

How-to instructions explain how you can build or make something. They often include numbered steps, pictures that help explain the steps, and a list of materials or ingredients that a reader will need. You can write how-to instructions for any type of process or procedure, from building a birdhouse to baking a cake. Other how-to ideas include writing instructions on how to play a computer game or a favorite sport, directions on the best route to take to school, or step-by-step instructions on the best way to study for a test.

Opinion Survey

An opinion survey is a way to collect different people's opinions on a particular topic. To create an opinion survey, the writer should come up with a question to ask. For example: Do you think there should be homework? Who is your favorite football player? What is your favorite flavor of ice cream? Once the writer has the question, he interviews a wide range of people to get their opinion. The writer collects all the answers and writes down what each person says word for word. The survey should include the participants' names next to their answers. Sometimes a picture of the person is included as well. Questions for opinion surveys can be on almost any topic that you can think of.

Song Lyrics

Song lyrics are a type of poetry. Songs can be a way of telling a story or expressing a feeling. There are two main parts to a song—the verse and chorus. A song will usually have two or three verses. Each verse is usually seven or eight lines and tells part of a story. The chorus retells the main idea of the song and will often repeat words and lines. The chorus may repeat three or four times in a song, in between each verse. Try writing some songs for a favorite artist or about a subject that interests you. Collect them to create an album. (Albums usually feature between 8 and 12 songs.) Come up with a title for the album and design a cover.

Advice Columns

In advice columns, readers write to the author of the column explaining their problems and asking for advice. The author responds with ideas to help the readers solve their problems. Some advice columnists, such as Dear Abby and Ann Landers, answer any kind of question. Other advice columnists answer questions about specific topics, such as car repair, gardening, or money management. Try writing an advice column about a topic you know a lot about. It can be anything from school to skateboarding.

Interviews

Interviews are similar to conversations. One person is asking questions and the other person is answering, usually giving information or opinions on a subject. When the interviewer is writing down the person's answers, it is important that he or she write down exactly what the other person has said.

Rebus Stories

Rebus stories are short stories with a little something special in them. In some places in the story, words are replaced with pictures. The reader has to "read" the pictures to make sense of the story. In some rebus stories, two or more pictures are used to represent a word, and the reader has to combine the sounds of the words to figure out what the word is.

Brochures

Brochures are written to give people information. They might tell people about a certain place or a certain subject. Usually they are small, often a sheet of paper folded in half or in thirds. Brochures can include written descriptions, diagrams, maps, or directions on building the subject.

Quizzes

Quizzes are fun ways for readers to test their knowledge on a certain subject. A quiz can be on any topic, from a test of sports knowledge to whether you are a good friend. The questions can be multiple choice or true or false. The quiz should include an answer key at the end.

Informational Articles

Informational articles are nonfiction stories that give readers new ideas or facts about a subject. The information is presented in well-organized formats. In some informational articles the writer presents an opinion on a subject and in each paragraph offers evidence that supports the opinion. An informational article can cover any subject that interests you.

Joke Collections

Just as people publish collections of favorite poems, people also publish collections of favorite jokes. Often an author will collect jokes on a certain theme, such as knock-knock jokes or jokes about school, and put them together in a collection. Adding illustrations to accompany the jokes can make the collection even more fun.

Postcards

Postcards are a quick way to present a snapshot and a brief bit of information. Postcards are usually about a famous person, place, or landmark. One side of the postcard should feature an illustration or picture of the person, place, or object. The back side is blank, except for the top left corner where there is a brief description of the picture. Add a short message to a friend on the postcard.

Profiles

A profile is a piece of writing that tells you about a person's life. A profile may include information about the subject's family, activities she likes to do, a list of her favorite things, and important events in her life. The profile could also include personal facts about the person, such as her age, weight, height, birthdate, and so on. Many times a picture will be included in the profile.

Reviews

A review is a person's opinion about how good or bad they think something is. Reviews can be written about books, records, shows, games, anything! Reviewers have taken the time to read, watch, or listen to something and share with other people what they think about it. But a reviewer can't just say that something is good or bad; he or she must use examples to back up the opinion. For example, if a reviewer thought a book was boring, he must give his reasons for thinking it boring.

Scrapbooks

Scrapbooks are collections of pictures and writing that people put together to remember special events. Scrapbooks can feature photographs with captions that describe what was happening in the picture. They can also include clippings from magazines and newspapers. You can create a scrapbook that records a special event in your life or one that describes the life of a fictional character or famous figure in history.

Cumulative Stories

 Cumulative stories follow a pattern. Each new line adds a new thought before repeating everything that went before. The reader of a cumulative story will notice that each new page will have more type than the page before.

Examples of cumulative stories include:
• *The Book That Jack Wrote* by Jon Scieszka (Viking, 1994)
• *The Judge* by Harve Zemach (Farrar, Straus and Giroux, 1969)

Character-based Stories

 In character-based stories, the focus is on the characters. In fact, these stories often contain little action. These stories may talk about what the characters are like or what they do. Each page tells us more and more about the characters. Often, character-based stories may focus on the relationship between characters.

Character-based stories include:
• *Rosie and Michael* by Judith Viorst (Aladdin Books, 1974)
• *The Giving Tree* by Shel Silverstein (Harper and Row, 1964)

Problem Stories

 In problem stories, an event or problem is presented at the beginning of the story, and the rest of the story is centered on how the characters will solve the problem.

An example of a problem story is:
• *What Do You Do With a Kangaroo?* by Mercer Mayer (Four Winds Press, 1973)

Interlocking Stories

 Interlocking stories follow a pattern. Each page of an interlocking story builds on what is said on the previous page. Sometimes interlocking stories are called "One thing leads to another" stories. The difference between interlocking stories and pattern stories is that interlocking stories do not repeat the same line of text on each page.

Examples of interlocking stories include:
• *If You Give a Mouse a Cookie* by Laura Jaffe Numeroff (Scholastic, 1985)
• *What Good Luck! What Bad Luck!* by Remy Charlip (Scholastic, 1969)

Circular Stories

Circular stories start with a character facing a problem in one location. As the story progresses, the character faces many obstacles and goes through many events, often exciting, in trying to solve the problem or reach a goal. In the end, the character is able to solve the problem, or reach his goal, and ends up back where he started.

Examples of circular stories include:
• *Could Be Worse* by James Stevenson (Mulberry Books, 1977)
• *Over the Steamy Swamp* by Paul Geraghty (Arrow Books, Ltd., 1988)

Tales with a Twist

Tales with a twist take favorite tales, such as a fairy tale or a folktale, and add new twists to them. The twist may be that the setting or time period has been changed, the characters may have changed, or the tale maybe told from a different point of view.

Examples of tales with a twist include:
• *Ruby* by Michael Emberley (Little, Brown & Co. 1990)
• *Snow White in New York* by Fiona French (Oxford University Press, 1986)

Concept Books

Concept books are often the first books that we learn to read. Counting books and ABC books are two of the most common types. Other kinds include books about opposites or place. While these books are often created for young readers, when a writer takes a creative approach to them, they can entertain readers of all ages.

Examples of concept books include:
• *Anamalia* by Graeme Base (Irwin Publishing, 1987)
• *The Yucky Reptile Alphabet Book* by Jerry Pallotta (Charlesbridge Pub,)

Repeating Pattern Stories

A repeating pattern story is one that has lines or phrases that are repeated on each page. New thoughts and ideas are added to each page, but the same sentence is repeated on each page. The repeated line can be used to start or end a new paragraph.

Examples of repeating pattern stories include:
• *The Important Book* by Margaret Wise Brown (Harper, 1960)
• *Alexander and the Terrible, Horrible, No Good, Very Bad Day* by Judith Viorst (Atheneum Press, 1972)

Tall Tales

What are Tall Tales, and how did they come to be?

A tall tale is a story that includes exaggeration. Many tall tales first appeared during the 1800s in the United States. At this time, people were settling new areas of the country. The land they were settling was thick, dark forest filled with bears and panthers; treeless plains; huge, mysterious mountains; and uncharted seacoasts.

The heroes and heroines of the tales often had exaggerated characteristics, making them able to tackle the dangers of the land.

As these stories were told around campfires and passed on from generation to generation, they became more and more exaggerated until they were unbelievable. In fact, some tall tales started out as stories about real people, such as Davy Crocket and Johnny Appleseed. Over time the characters' daring feats were more and more exaggerated until eventually the characters grew into heroes and heroines of tall tales. These stories often provided humor and entertainment after a long hard day, but they also helped the pioneers and settlers face their own challenges in the environment.

Features of a Tall Tale

Setting: The stories take place in the past. Often they take place in the wilderness or in a small town. Rarely would you find a tall tale taking place in a big city.

Characters: Most of the time the heros/heroines are exaggerated characters. Possibly it is their physical appearance or their capabilities (what they can do) that are exaggerated. The main character may be a pioneer or settler, explorer, sea captain, firefighter, farmer, cowboy, cowgirl, railroad worker, logger, and so on. It is important to start a tall tale off with a detailed description of the hero/heroine.

The Story: After the character is introduced, the reader learns about a problem facing the character. Usually the problem involves a force of nature, such as panthers, bears, and other animals, or cyclones, tornadoes, the wind, or other weather. The force may be taking something, preventing something, frightening people, or challenging the hero directly. The remainder of the story describes the plan the hero uses to overcome the force. (It may be through a challenge, contest, or a plan to defeat the force.) Often there is more than one attempt to defeat the force. All attempts are exaggerated (wrestling panthers and roping the wind are characteristic examples).

The Ending: The ending of the tall tale usually explains how the hero or heroine defeats the force and what becomes of the force. In some stories a natural feature is formed due to a battle.

Part Two

Sharpening Skills

Students are usually excited to get started when they begin writing. They enthusiastically gather ideas and start to view the world around them as a potential source for stories. However, if we truly wish to see our students develop as writers, we need for them to understand the importance of using proper punctuation and grammar and of developing their vocabulary.

Often students see this as the dry or boring part of writing. Writers want to get on with writing. That is why it is important to emphasize to children that these activities will help them further develop as writers. Once students realize there is value for them in these activities, they become actively involved. When they are comfortable with the writing process, I begin to incorporate mini-lessons on punctuation, grammar, and vocabulary in our writing class. These mini-lessons are described in this section.

Mini–Lesson 5 Punctuation: The Traffic Signs of Writing

I begin with a mini-lesson reviewing basic punctuation. I hand out to students copies of the reproducible Punctuation: The Traffic Signs of Writing (page 28). I also hang a poster in the classroom that lists the basic punctuation rules.

To reinforce students' knowledge of punctuation, I follow-up with the Proofreader's Challenges (pages 29–37). These are a series of short stories that students can use to practice their punctuation skills and familiarize themselves with the editing process. I created these pieces after I realized that students were reluctant to be critical of their own work. They had invested so much time in their writing that they viewed any criticism as a reflection of the quality of the ideas and even of themselves rather than of the mechanics of their pieces. Students felt more at ease correcting these generic pieces. And they learned firsthand that editing is not a judgment of the content. I used the Proofreader's Challenges over several weeks, usually giving students one a week. Answer keys for the Proofreader's Challenges appear at the back of the book (page 76–80).

Mini-Lesson **6** Don't Say . . .

After punctuation, the next skills lessons are on word choice and using a dictionary and thesaurus. To begin, I hand out copies of the Don't Say "Said" reproducible (page 38). After students have studied my example, I have them work in pairs and assign each pair an overused word. (With this activity, you can target words you find your students overusing.) Each pair then completes the Don't Say "___" reproducible (page 39) by finding as many alternatives to the word as possible. Students share their finished product with the class and then we post the results for students to use as a source for new words.

Additional Vocabulary-Building Activities

A twist on the Don't Say "Said" activity is to have students create I'm Talking posters, which feature an overused word and possible synonyms. For example:

> I'm talking good!
> I'm talking nice.
> I'm talking excellent, fine, likeable,
> Delightful!
> I'm talking swell, keen, dandy, great,
> I'm talking brilliant, superb, glorious,
> Impressive!
> I'm talking splendid, and pleasing,
> I'm talking good!

Another vocabulary-stretching activity is to have students brainstorm words for each of the five senses. An example might include:

Sight:	shimmering, glaring, hazy
Touch:	dull, sharp, soft
Taste:	tangy, bitter, savory
Hearing:	hushed, ear-splitting, thunderous
Smell:	pungent, aromatic, fragrant

Don't Say . . .

Some possible word choices to provide students. These are often overused words.

good	ugly	scary	tall
strong	strange	liked	sad
looked	small	hot	happy
bad	funny	nice	smart
rude	dirty	cold	mad
smelly	walked	pretty	
big	delicious	loud	

Mini–Lesson **7** Expanding Sentences

This activity (pages 40–41) helps students see how they can expand sentences by adding details. As we discuss how to do this, I review the vocabulary used to describe parts of speech, such as nouns, verbs, adverbs, and adjectives. I emphasize how it's important to learn the terms used in sentences because if we all use the same language it is easier for us to help each other.

Mini–Lesson **8** Combining Sentences

Inexperienced writers will often fill their stories with simple sentences. Offering a mini-lesson on combining simple sentences, helps give students the skills to address this problem when they are revising their own stories. Combining Sentences (page 42) lets students practice combining a series of simple sentences into paragraphs of more complex and interesting sentences.

Mini–Lesson **9** Using Dialogue

Dialogue is what makes a story come alive, but students often have difficulty incorporating dialogue in their writing. This mini-lesson (page 43) addresses the conventions of writing dialogue, including using quotation marks and starting new dialogue on new lines.

Name _____

Punctuation: The Traffic Signs of Writing

Imagine if the roads that we drive our cars on had no traffic signs or traffic lights? People would be driving their cars everywhere, not knowing when to stop or where to go. It would be very confusing!

Periods, commas, colons, and other punctuation marks operate like traffic signs and lights for readers. They tell us when to stop, when to slow down, and when to keep going. When writers use the correct punctuation, they are helping readers travel through their writing.

Here are some of the main types of punctuation that a writer can use:

The Period

A period is like a stop sign. It is placed at the end of a sentence. The question a writer should ask is, "When do I need to stop?" To figure out where one sentence ends and another begins, look for the place where one idea or thought ends and a new one begins.

Often writers will have trouble with periods when they want to join more than one idea together. One of the best ways to know when to put in a period is to reread the writing out loud. If you need to stop and take a breath, then you know a period is needed.

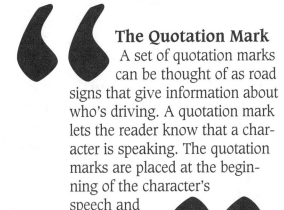

The Quotation Mark

A set of quotation marks can be thought of as road signs that give information about who's driving. A quotation mark lets the reader know that a character is speaking. The quotation marks are placed at the beginning of the character's speech and at the end.

The Comma

The comma can be thought of as a yield sign telling the reader to slow down. You can use a comma to join two complete ideas together, or several commas and a conjunction following the last when you are listing a series of items.

The Colon

The colon can be thought of as a warning sign. It tells the reader that there is more to come. Often you will place a colon just before you begin a list of items. It makes the reader stop and pay attention to what is coming.

Proofreader's Challenge
Walking Down Fig Street

Have you been very afraid of something, only to find out later that it wasn't scary at all? Well let me tell you about a time I did just that.

In september I started at a new school. Soon i found the shortest way to get my new school. I would walk across a empty feild, down a back lane and turn on to a tiny little street called fig street and that would take me to the school parking lot. i liked going this way cause it seemed that no, other kids walked this way to school. It gave me a chance to be by myself and instead of walking with a large group of kids.

After the first few weeks I notices that I was'nt walking my faverite path alone. Each morning as I came out of the back lane and turned onto Fig Street I heard footsteps behind me. The first time I didnt think much of it and as I got to the end of the street the footsteps disaapeared. Now you may wonder why I didn't just turn around and look. The truth was that I was to scared too.

Everyday after I turn on Fig street I would hear the foot steps behind me. Each day I became a little braver and I would turn my head slitly and look over my shulder. At first all I saw was a long shadow. The next time I turned my head, I could see a figere was dressed in black.

Little by little, I saw more of the figere. It appeared to have a black hood and long black robe. The footsteps moved so slowly they made me nervous.

Finally I couldn'nt take it none more. I decided the next day I would face the figere.

The next morning, as i turned on to fig Street, I heard the footsteps again. This time the footsteps slowed down, as if the figere was ready to pounce. And so I turned around and scremed at the figere, "STOP FOLLOWING ME."

Imagine my horror an emberesment, as I found myself facing an elderly nun who was out for her dayly walk.

Proofreader's Challenge
The Statue

once upun a time in a land far far away they're lived a king king clement's wife had died many years ago and left him with one daughter Princess Elizabeth was the most presieus thing to king Clement whatever his daughter wanted king clement would give her one day the King announced that a new statue would be shown at the courtyard fountain on the opening day of the county fare soon all the townspeple were talking about the statue to be place in the courtyard stories were spreading that was the king's daughter princess Elizabeth herself who had made it.

while all this talk was going on peter the Baker was out of town and did not her the storyies on the day of the fair everybody gathered in the castle courtyard music was playing games were set up and food served halfway through the celebretion trumpets sounded as the king unveiled the statue for the towns fountain.

When the statue was uncovered the crowd oohed and awed and clapped and cheered "beautiful" yealled a group of woman "superb" called the men at the back now the strange thing about this all was that the statue was quite ugly of courze since everybody knew who made it but nobody dared say anything bad in fear of the kings anger. All but poor Peter the baker who did not know this he laughed out loud and exclaimed "We can't put that thing in the couryard, its emeressing.

the whole crowd went silent and they turned to the king standing on the steps of the castle everybody waited to hear the order for Peter to be thrown in the dungun the king spoke slowly "come here young man" Peter went to stand next to the king my loyel subject said the king my daughter and I have played a little trick we wished to see if people would be honest with us we brought out this hideous statue and had everybody believe my daughter make it but her is her real one the guards brought out a statue that was remarkeable this young man, said the King, was the only person who was honest with us he shown me he can be trusted in fact trusted enough to have my daughter's hand in marriage after that peter was not known as Peter the baker anymore.

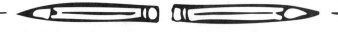

Proofreader's Challenge
Mr. Singular

mr. Singular was a man of habit. He liked things to be same each and every day. This way he knew what to expected. He ate his supper at the same time each day, visit his mother each Sunday, and clean his house on fridays after the work week ended.

One of Mr. Singulaar's favorite habits was to walk to work. Each day he wake up a little earlier than necessary so he could walk threw the park on his way to work. halfway through he would stop at the same park bench sit and read his morning paper and eat his muffiin.

Now the other importent thing to know about Mr. Singular was that he was a very loneley man. You see other than his mother Mr. singular had know other family or friends he could visit. You mite be wandering why this was so but the simpel fact was that Mr. Singular just did'nt feel comforteable around people. He tired joining a stamp club but felt akwerd around all them others, who knew so much more then him, he tried writing pen pal letters but did'nt know what to say. So finaly Mr. Singular gave up trying and instead just wished for a freind.

His dayly path to work remeinded him how lonely was he. He past the small pond, and wished he had someone to go fishing with, he walked by the baseball feild and wished he had some to play ball with he passed the man who fed the birds each day and wished he had a friend to share things with, and he saw people chatting at the bus stop and wished he had someone to talk too.

Proofreader's Challenge
Mr. Singular (Part 2)

One day Mr. Singular noticed something different about his usuall moring walk. The man who feeded the birds was not at his usuall spot.

how strange thought Mr. Singular. He is here eveery day giving bread crums to the birds. What could have happened to him!

Just then the bird feeding man slowly walked up the path with his hands in his pockets. He plopped down on the bench next to Mr. Singular and sighed. teh man looked so disterbed that Mr. Singular did not even think about being uncomfortable when he asked. is something the matter?

"oh yes" the man replied. You see each day I save bread crumbs to bring the birds. But somehow this morning all my cupboards were bear. I dodn't half a single scrap and it is to early for the stores to be open. My poor feathered friends will have to go with out for the first time today.

Mr. Singular looked down at his muffin, "Here use this, I'm sure the birds will love it".

"But this is your brekfast" said the man. That's okay said mr. Singular. The next day when Mr. Singular sat on his usual bench the man appeared again, this time with bread crums and two muffins.

The two men meet each morning to feed the birds. Soon after there first convercation the berd man suggested they meet at the pond in the park on saterday and go fishing. The following weekend they met at the park to play ball.

Sometimes what we wish for is staring at us all we need to do is notice it.

Proofreader's Challenge
The Revenge of Johnny Cupcake

Every skool has a child that is considred the school bully. There is that one student that tererizes every body. At Franklin elementary Schkool that bullie was Meatbone Malone. Meatbone recieved this name for of his reputashun for chewing on huge meatbones in the lunchroom. rumurs flew that some of these meatbones were former students. Of course everybody new this was false but it added to the legend of meatbone malone.

They're were many storys about meatbone Malone that were told to new studnets including the day he tied a boys shoelases to the flagpole with the boy still wearing the shoes, and the time he stole a pear of glasses from a girl. But the famousest tale was about the day Meatbone Malone met up with Little Johnny Cupcake.

Now this was not Johnny's real name. But once in the lunchroom Meatbone seen Johnny with a cupcake, and sqiushed the cupcake in his face and desided that Little Johnny Cupcake was johnny's new nickname. Johnny was small boy, with big thick glasses, red hair, and many frekles. Johnny always had his nose in a book, he was just the kind a studnet Meatbone loved to pick on.

One day Johnny was walking to he's class, reading a book wile he walkt. he was pre-ocupied because his African violet floweres were wilting and Johnny was searching for a solushun to his dilema. As he read through his book someone banged into him. Wham! his glasses and book fell to the floor. Of course Johnny being allready upset about his flowers did not stop to think, and blurtted out Watch where your going you clumsy ox.

When Johnny put on his glasses he could see two huge feet next to him. He looked way up to see the dasterdly smile of Meatbone Malone. A hushed fell in the hall.

Proofreader's Challenge
The Revenge of Johnny Cupcake (Part 2)

Everyone new this was the end for Johnny Cupcake. No one dared tawk back to Meatbone, not ever.

Johnny jump to his feet and started running. He knew his only chance was eskap. Meatbone thundered a long behind.

Johnny turned the corner and reached a dead end the only thing to do was duck into the boys bathroom. Johnny baked against the wall and trembled. BOOM BOOM the footsteps aproched and the pane of glass on the door rattled. The bathroom door flew open and their stood huge shadowy bulk of Meatbone Malone.

Johnny pressed himself against the mirrors on the back wall of the bathroom as meatbone stepped closer and closer. Just as Johnny could feel the hot air blowing out of Meatbone's nostrels, the bully stopped, looked up into the mirror and froze. he started backing up further and further and then raced out of the bathroom.

What Meatbone had seen in the mirror that day so the story goes washis own relfection surrounded by fiery flames. In fact it was such a hideous site that Meatbone transfered schools later that day. Thats how terrified he was.

The part of the legend that has nevered been told and only know to johnny was taht he was thankful he just finished reading about reflections in his encylopedia. Little johnny used his flame red marble to reflect against the bathroom taps and onto the bathroom mirror.

Sometimes brains can beat brawn.

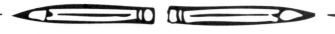

Proofreader's Challenge
Buddy and Sweetie

The best Summer I'd ever had was the year I met Buddy and sweetie i was elevin years old that summer, and I'l never forget it.

It did not start out in such a postitively way. Just before the end of school year my dad gots a announcement fromm his job saying that we would have to move to australia to open a new office for his company my dad sold inshurence, whatever that is.

one night at dinner Mamma and daddy disscussed our familys' plans. At the beginning of school vacashun Mama and Daddy would fly to australia. Daddy would set up his new office while Mama would search for a new house for us i will be going to spend the Summer with Grandpa and Grandma.

I was very sad about this news. I loved my grandpa and Grandma but they lived on a farm far away from any other kids. They're would be no one to play with what does a elevin year old girl have in comon witha seventy year old cuple I thought.

But there was no use mowning about it plans were set. I would be on the farm all summer until Mama returned to pick me up. the day Mama droped me off at my Granparents farm was a very uncomfortable day. I was ver polight to them but they seemed like strangers. Since they lived so far away I never spent much time with them, I felt very gloomey watching my mother drive away leaving me with these too anchent people.

Proofreader's Challenge
Buddy and Sweetie (Part 2)

That first night Grandma and Grandpa tried to help me get used to the place Grandma made a supper that I must admit smelled dlishious Grandpa kept on trying to tell jokes but couldn't remember the endings. I couldnt help but laugh but I was still sad.

I had been in bed, what seemed like only a short time when I felt a knudge on my sholder. It was Grandpa with a flashlite in his hand, all dressed. He told me to get my cloths and follow them to the barn. It was four oclock in the morning

Once inside the barn Grandpa tooked me to two pens where horses stretched out on hey. A man who I later found out was an animal dockter was there Grandpa infomred me that the horses was ready to give birth and if i wanted the babies could be mine. I was amased.

When the sun cam up that morning I was the owner for a male and a female horse. I named them Buddy and Sweetie. For the rest of the summer i spent my days with Buddy and Sweetie. A day ususally went as follows feed the horses, take them for they're morning walk, groom them, feed them again, walk them again, and then let them rest with their mothers.

by the end of the summer i was totally attached to the horse and to my grandparents as well. I made a promise that each summer vaction I would return to see my grandparents and my horses.

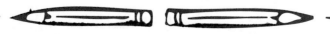

Proofreader's Challenge
Digger's Mistake

Once apon a time there was two dogs that lived by side by side as nieghbers over many years the too dogs spend much time together. playing ball, going for walks and barking at cats. Other dogs considerd the two good friends.

Now max was the bigger of them two dogs and greatly admired by others who said he could have been a show dog, Digger was smaller, and a runt of a dog and could never do things quit as well as Max. he could not run as fast or bark as lowd. Max new which postman to bark at, and how to stay away form the dogcatchers. Digger admired max and would do anything for his friend.

One day Max receved a new blanket from his masters. He put it in his doghouse and went for a stroll in the afternoon when he returned he find digger in his dog house sleeping on the new blanket. Now it was not that Digger meaned to take something from his friend, he just wanted to share something that belonged to his dear dear friend. He knewed he should have have asked but sometimes dogs make mistakes.

Digger apologized over and over to his friend but Max said told him him to leave. For days Digger never seen his friend. He no longer had anyone to play ball, to chase cats with or to bark with. A few more days past and then Max stopped by wondering if digger wanted to go to the park.

Of course digger said yes he missed his friend so much Max said he had missed Digger to.

digger was relieved that Max finally understand that sometimes mistakes happen.

Don't Say "_____," Say . . .

Expanding Sentences

All English sentences have two essential parts: a subject and a predicate. For example, "Janine is running." is a sentence. The diagram below shows that some sentences give us the same information, but go one step further by giving us more details. Examine each sentence and make yourself familiar with the way a sentence works.

Sentence

The   dog   chased   the   ball.

subject

A subject is a noun or pronoun that is the "doer" of the sentence.

predicate (verb)

The predicate tells what the subject does.

direct object

The direct object is the noun or pronoun that recieves the action.

Expanded Sentence

The   scruffy   mutt   wildly   chased   the   bitten-up   ball.

subject   predicate   direct object

adjective

An adjective describes what noun is like; it adds detail.

noun

adverb

An adverb describes the kind of of action. Often adverbs will end in -ly.

verb

adjective

This adjective describes the direct object.

noun

Expanding Sentences (Part 2)

Change each of the following sentences by using adverbs and adjectives. You may wish to trade in the nouns and verbs in each sentence for more interesting ones.

The boy spilled his milk on the floor.

_____

_____

The kite's string broke in the wind.

_____

_____

The street is slippery.

_____

_____

The dog ripped the pages of the book.

_____

_____

The sun melted the chocolate bar.

_____

_____

Combining Sentences

Often when we write we use short sentences to tell each idea, but when we read the sentences back they do not sound very natural. The reason for this is that when we speak or read something, we combine ideas together.

When you are writing a first draft, it is okay to use short sentences. Once you start to revise your work, you should try joining (or combining) sentences to get a more natural-sounding type of writing.

Here is an example:

Timmy has a dog. It's name is Fluffy. It is black and brown. The dog has soft fur. Timmy loves his dog. He follows Timmy everywhere. Timmy likes to give treats to his dog. Fluffy stands up and barks for them.

You shouldn't try to combine all of these sentences, but you should look for ideas that fit together. You can use commas and conjunctions to connect sentences. Here's how these short sentences can be combined.

Timmy's pet, Fluffy, is a black and brown dog with soft fur. Timmy loves his dog and everywhere Timmy goes, the dog follows along. Fluffy stands up and barks when Timmy gives him a treat.

Now see if you can combine some of the following sentences.

Jane is a young girl. She is beautiful. She has curly black hair. She has dark brown eyes. Everybody stares at her when she walks down the street. People say she looks like a princess. Jane is very embarrassed.

_____

_____

_____

_____

The siren went off. It was loud. The whole neighborhood could hear it. Two men ran out of a building. It was the building with the siren. They were carrying a big bag. The men had masks on their faces. The police came. They started chasing the two men.

_____

_____

_____

_____

REMEMBER: When you combine sentences, you can change the order of words as long as they still make sense.

Using Dialogue

Dialogue is conversation in writing. Having characters talk to one another makes a story more believable. There are useful rules to follow when writing dialogue.

Read the story below.

>   Stella and Sherri decided to go shopping for decorations for their big summer party. What do you think we should buy? I don't know. Well what about this? Gee, I don't know if they would go with all the other decorations. Well they are the right color. Okay. Let's get them. The two girls went to the cash register.

What's wrong with this story?

The following conventions, or rules, for using dialogue would make this story easier to read.

- Use quotation marks (" ") around the words that a person speaks.

- Start a new line each time a different character begins speaking (regardless of where the previous line ended).

- Introduce or follow dialogue with words such as said, replied, commented, remarked, and so on, along with the speaker's name.

- Include details that further explain why characters are saying what they say.

Here's a revised story using some of these tips.

>   Stella and Sherri decided to go shopping for decorations for their summer party. As they entered the store, Stella asked, "What do you think we should buy?"
>
>   "I don't know," said Sherri in a puzzled voice.
>
>   "Well, what about this?" replied Stella, as she held up a bag of yellow balloons.
>
>   "Gee, I don't know if they would go with all the other decorations. Well, they are the right color," Sherri remarked.
>
>   "Okay. Let's get them," replied Stella. The two girls went to the cash register.

Now that you see how proper dialogue can be written, try writing some dialogue yourself. Write a scene with two children in a park deciding what they should play.

Part Three

Exploring the Elements of Writing

Simply engaging a student in the writing process does not ensure that a student will become a good writer. Students need to study and explore the elements of good writing. Just as a painter learns about mixing colors and types of brush strokes, so too, does a writer need to know how words combine and behave in order to use them effectively.

The elements of good writing include deciding on a point of view for a story, constructing a plot, determining the story's setting, developing interesting characters, crafting compelling leads and endings, and using figurative language. The following mini-lessons are designed to show students how to incorporate these elements as they revise and edit their stories.

Mini-Lesson 10 Point of View: First and Third Person

One of the first decisions a writer must make is who will be telling the story. Will the writer use a first-person or a third-person narrator? To help students understand this concept, I use the First Person and Third Person reproducible (page 47). I review the terms with students, and together we read "A Tale Told in Two" and discuss the different points of view. We might also discuss stories we have read in class that have first- or third-person narrators.

Next, I have students craft a short story with a first-person narrator, using the Understanding Point of View reproducible on page 48. For the purposes of this activity, the story can be quite simple, just an opening scene of a story or even a brief description of a part of a school day. Once students have completed their stories, I collect them and redistribute them to the class. Students must then take the new story they have received and rewrite it using a third-person narrator. I return the stories to the original writers, who can then compare the two versions of the story.

Mini-Lesson **11** Setting: Where It All Happens

Students will often include the setting of their stories in the first paragraph and never mention it again. To encourage students to think about the setting of their stories and how it can affect them, we use the reproducible lesson Setting: Where It All Happens (pags 49–50). Students use this page as prompt and as a way to plan and shape the setting of their stories.

Mini-Lesson **12** Setting: Making an Illustration

In this lesson (pages 51–52), students are asked to write a descriptive paragraph about the setting of a story. This can be a story they are currently working on or a new story created for this activity. Then I ask students to exchange paragraphs with one another and draw an illustration of the other person's setting. Students can confer with the writer about the illustration, which will help the writer see what additional details he or she could add to create a clearer picture of the setting.

Mini-Lesson **13** Leads: How to Get the Story Going

Crafting a compelling lead is an important skill for any writer. This lesson (pages 53–54) introduces students to five different kinds of leads they can use and then challenges them to write an example of each kind of lead.

Mini-Lesson **14** Character: A Day in the Life...

Most student work is plot driven. Students are often under the misconception that the more events a story has, the better it will be. But often, the best-loved books are character driven. It is the ability to identify with a character and his actions and feelings that commit us to a story.

Writing a character study is one way for students to work on characterization. In this lesson, students pick any adult they know (the reproducible directs them to choose an adult who works in your school), and imagine what that person was like as a kid. To prompt their thinking, they complete the A Day in the Life reproducible (page 55). Then they use this information about their character to write a short story.

Mini-Lesson **15** Character: Reactions

In this lesson (pages 56–57), students explore how incorporating character reaction in a story helps a reader learn about the characters. Students begin by reading two versions of a story and comparing how the character's reactions to a situation change the story. Then they can try crafting their own examples.

Mini-Lesson **16** Plot: Chain-Reaction Maps

The plot of any story is moved along by how characters react to certain events. A story will often begin with an event to which a character then reacts, which leads in turn to another event. Use the Chain Reaction Maps (pages 58–59) to help students understand how a chain of events, and the character's reactions to each event, shape a story.

Mini-Lesson **17** Language: Showing vs. Telling

This lesson demonstrates to students how good writers show readers what is happening instead of simply telling them. Hand out copies of the mini-lesson reproducibles (pages 60–61). You may wish to reproduce the first page on an overhead transparency and review the examples with the class before having students complete the second part of the reproducible.

Mini-Lesson **18** Language: Adding Details

After completing a first draft of a story, it's helpful for writers to go back to their stories to find places where they can add more details that will make scenes vivid to readers. In this mini-lesson (pages 62–63), students explore how adding details makes a story more interesting.

Mini-Lesson **19** Language: Simile Characters

Encourage students to use figurative language and study the language around them by having them create simile characters. Review similes with students using the Simile Character reproducible (page 64), then have them create their own simile characters. These characters can be created on large sheets of paper and displayed in the classroom.

Mini-Lesson **20** Endings: Put a Finishing Touch on Your Story

Inexperienced writers will often abruptly end their stories. By examining how other authors wrap up their stories, students learn how they can wrap-up stories successfully. The reproducible The End: Put a Finishing Touch on Your Story (page 65) features examples of effective last lines.

First Person and Third Person

One of the important things to notice about a story is who's telling it. Sometimes it's a first-person narrator. This means an "I" is telling us a story about something that happened to him or her. Remember that in a fiction story told in first person, the "I" is not the author. The "I" is a person the author has created to tell the story. First-person narrators can only describe what they personally see, hear, and know. They can't get into the other characters' minds and tell what's going on there.

Other times, authors use third-person narration. In a third-person story, the narrator who is telling the story isn't the voice of one of the characters. The third-person narrator is an all-knowing voice who can see what is happening to different characters and what they see, know, and feel. It is the voice that says "she did this" or "he felt that." When you read, notice which narrative voice the author has chosen. Think about why an author might choose this voice. How would the story have been different if the voice had been changed?

When you are writing, you pick a narrative voice before you even put the pen to paper.

A Tale Told in Two

First Person

One bright sunny morning, I was on my way to school. I was in good mood—a sunny day always makes me happy. I noticed the birds singing and thought the birds must look forward to such bright cheerful days too. Little did I know that the day would soon turn dark for me.

As I was walking down the street, enjoying my morning stroll, I noticed a square, brown thing lying on the curb of the road. At first, I thought it was probably nothing more than some litter. But as I got closer, I could see it was a fairly expensive-looking wallet and not the kind of thing that would be thrown away. I bent down to pick it up, and right away I could tell it was full of something. To my amazement, it contained a wad of hundred dollar bills. I stared at the money and right then I heard someone screaming from down the street. "Stop thief! Stop," called a man. I wondered what was going on. Then I noticed that the man was running towards me!

Third Person

One bright sunny morning, Jimmy was on his way to school. He appeared to be in good spirits as the sun shone. A bright sunny day always lifted Jimmy's spirits. He noticed the birds singing and studied them carefully. Little did Jimmy know that his day would soon turn dark.

As he was walking down the street, enjoying his morning stroll, he noticed a square, brown object lying on the side of the road. At first, Jimmy thought nothing of it as he walked by, assuming it was just discarded trash. But as Jimmy got closer he could tell it was an expensive wallet. He bent down to pick it up and knew by the weight that it was filled with something. Inside he discovered a wad of hundred dollar bills. Jimmy was too stunned to notice the man running down the street towards him. It wasn't until he heard the words, "Stop, thief! Stop!" that Jimmy turned and saw the man coming towards him!

Understanding Point of View

Part 1:
Write a First-Person Story

Reading the stories about the boy Jimmy, you can see how the same tale can be told in two ways. In the first example, the author has written it from Jimmy's point of view.

Take some time to write a short story using a first-person narrator. Imagine you are a character to whom something surprising has just happened. In your short story tell how the character (you) is feeling and thinking about the event.

_____

_____

_____

_____

_____

_____

_____

Part 2:
Write a Third-Person Story

Now you'll have the chance to write a third-person story, but not your own! You will be given someone else's first-person story. See if you can turn another writer's story into a third-person version.

First read through the story carefully. Think about what the character is feeling, thinking, and saying. How can you rewrite it so that you show the character's thoughts and behavior without speaking in the character's voice? Keep the first-person version next to you as you write your third-person version. Be sure you include all the important details and try not to change the events.

You will be turning your finished version over to the original writer, and someone will be handing you a version of your first-person story transformed into the third person. See what you think about the two versions.

_____

_____

_____

_____

_____

_____

_____

Setting: Where It All Happens

It is important to explain where and when a story takes place. A good setting is one in which a reader can always imagine where the characters are at any time in the story. Use the following questions to plan and develop a good setting for your story.

Step 1: Decide on the main location(s) for the story. Where will your main characters spend most of their time? Describe this setting. What does it look like? What special features does it contain? You may want to mention small details about this setting throughout your story.

_____

_____

_____

_____

_____

_____

Step 2: Make some choices. Is there going to be one main setting where most of the events take place, or will there be many different locations? If there are many, start making a list of some of these sites. Once you have planned out your setting, look back at your notes. Decide which details of the setting a reader needs to know right from the beginning. Then start to number other details in the order they need to be introduced.

_____

_____

_____

_____

_____

_____

Setting: Where It All Happens (Part 2)

Step 3: Decide if your story will take place in a real location or if you will use a fictional setting. If you decide on using a real place, you may want to do some research before you begin your story. What does the location look like? Are there special features? What real place names can you use? What is the weather like?

   If you decide on a fictional setting, you may want to write a description of the place. How large or small is the location? What types of structures are there? What types of place names will you need for your story?

_____

_____

_____

_____

Step 4: Pick a time. When will your story take place? If your story takes place in the present, are there real-life events that you can incorporate? If your story takes place in the past, research that time period to make your descriptions as authentic as possible. If your story takes place in the future, what special elements or features will exist?

_____

_____

_____

_____

Step 5: Find the most descriptive details. Once you've planned out your setting, look back at your notes. Decide which details of the setting are the most vivid and let your readers clearly imagine the story's location. How can you improve descriptions that aren't very clear or precise? Find words that turn your description into a believable word-picture.

_____

_____

_____

_____

As you write your story, keep this setting outline by your side. Include details of the setting into the story where they seem to fit.

Imagining the Setting of a Story

Did you know that most picture books are not illustrated by the writer? Usually an illustrator is hired to create the artwork for the text. In fact, the illustrator may create the artwork without ever having spoken to the author. She will read the author's description and then imagine what the setting and the characters look like.

This is one reason why it is so important for the author to use words wisely in describing details. And since the illustrator—and readers—want to know where the action of the story is taking place, it is important for the writer to include many details about the story's setting.

Imagining the Setting as an Author

Imagine that a book company has requested that you write a story about a young child (boy or girl) who gets involved in a wild and exciting adventure. However, before you begin writing the story you must write a description of where the story will take place so that an illustrator can start on a sketch for the cover.

Picture the setting you want your story to have. Then write a detailed paragraph that describes the setting. Remember to include any important elements that will be mentioned in your story. The paragraph should be so descriptive that a reader could easily picture the setting.

_____

_____

_____

_____

_____

_____

_____

_____

_____

_____

Imagining the Setting of a Story (Part 2)

Imagining the Setting as an Illustrator

You have just been given a description of a story's setting from an author. Now you have to illustrate the setting for the book cover.

    First, you should read the description a few times. Try and picture a scene in your mind. Once you have some ideas, start illustrating. Refer back to the description if you are unsure of how something should be. You can use some of your own ideas and you can consult with the author to see how the author imagined the scene. Draw a picture of the setting below.

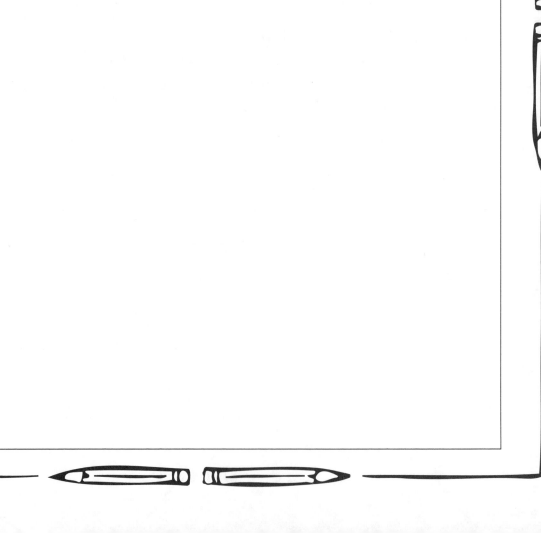

Leads: How to Get the Story Going

Leads are the beginning sentences of a story. A lead is the first impression a reader receives about your story, and it is often the way a writer draws readers in and convinces them to read more.

Here are some of the kinds of leads you can choose from.

• A Place in Time

This is one of the most successful types of leads and among the most commonly used. In the opening paragraph the writer describes when or where the story will take place. Some common lines used in such a lead include: "Once upon a time..." "Long, long ago..." "One bright, sunny day..." or "In a land far, far away..."

• It All Begins Here

Another way to get the reader quickly involved in the story is to start off with an event or some kind of action. Examples of this type of lead include: "Smash! The window cracked, the wind howled, and the door flung open..." or "The two cars backed up into each other..."

• The Character

Beginning a story by having a character speaking, thinking, or doing something is another type of lead. You can select one of three different kinds of character leads: a character speaking, a character thinking, or a character doing something.

Can you identify which type of lead is being used?

"But I don't want to go to the store," moaned Millie, when her mom stepped into the room making the request.

• _____

It's always me that gets stuck doing all the jobs around here, Millie thought to herself when her mom asked her to go the store.

• _____

Millie put on her coat and hat and then slammed the door behind her as she left for the store. Once again her mom had asked her to do an errand.

• _____

Leads: How to Get the Story Going (Part 2)

Now that you have learned about the possible leads a story can have, try and create five different leads for the same story. Here is a synopsis of the story:

> On a rainy day, two boys are walking home from school when they see a hot air balloon come crashing down in the park just ahead of them.

Write a(n):

Place-in-Time Lead

_____

_____

_____

It-All-Begins-Here Lead

_____

_____

_____

Character-Talking Lead

_____

_____

_____

Character-Thinking Lead

_____

_____

_____

Character-Doing Lead

_____

_____

_____

A Day Iin the Life of...

Although it's sometimes hard to imagine, everybody was once young. Your challenge is to select an adult who works in the school and imagine what he or she was like at your age.

Use the questions below as a guide for a story about what a typical day would have been like for that adult as a young person. Since your story is fiction, your information does not have to be correct; in fact, it can be as funny as you like. Include an illustration that shows what you think your subject would have looked like as a child. Finally, remember you are using a real person as a basis for your fiction, so be sensitive to the person's feelings.

1. What kind of house does the person live in? An apartment? A house? A farm house?

2. What kind of hobbies can you imagine the person having?

3. What kind of family does the person have? Is he or she an only child, the oldest in the family, or the youngest? Does the person have any pets?

4. What kind of student was the person at school? What subjects were his or her favorite and least favorite? Did the person ever get into any trouble?

5. What was the person's favorite television show, food, toys, and color? What type of clothing did he or she like to wear?

6. What would the person do outside of school—play games with friends? play on a team? play a musical instrument? ride his or her bike?

Try to include any other information you can think of. Then write a story that describes an ordinary day—from start to finish—for your subject.

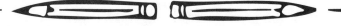

Character Reaction

When we read a book, we are interested in what the characters do. But if all we learn about them is what they do, we become bored very quickly. We also want to know what the characters feel and think. It is through both their actions and their reactions to an event that we learn who they are and how they feel.

Here is an example of a scene from a story with no character reaction. Notice how the first version is much shorter than the others and not as interesting.

Marcy was sitting at a restaurant table waiting for her friend, Lee, to join her. The place was crowded and filled with the noise of customers chatting, waiters and cooks calling out, and music playing. Lee had been anxious to try this new restaurant.

Twenty minutes passed and still no Lee. Marcy wondered where she was.

Here is a version of the story with character reactions included.

Marcy was sitting at a restaurant table waiting for her friend, Lee, to join her. The place was crowded and filled with the noise of customers chatting, waiters and cooks calling out, and music playing. Marcy felt uncomfortable with so many people around. She would have preferred having a small picnic at the park instead. However, Lee was anxious to try this new restaurant.

Twenty minutes passed and still no Lee. Marcy grew concerned. What could be holding her up? Marcy tried not to think of bad things because she knew she would grow worried. Yet, if nothing bad had happened, then where was Lee? It wasn't like her to be so late.

Now here is another version with the same character having a different reaction.

Marcy was sitting at a restaurant table waiting for her friend, Lee, to join her. The place was crowded and filled with the noise of customers chatting, waiters and cooks calling out, and music playing. Marcy loved the excitement and activity all around her, She bopped her head to the steady beat of the music and observed all the people. Lee had been very anxious to try this new restaurant and Marcy was glad she suggested it.

Twenty minutes passed and still no Lee. Marcy was not concerned. She did not mind waiting for her friend. If she wasn't there, then something must have come up. No doubt she would get there as soon as she could. Marcy wondered if Lee would have some exciting story to tell her.

Marcy is a very different character in each version. Her thoughts and feelings about what is going on around her tell us what she is like.

Character Reaction (Part 2)

Now see if you can create two different versions of the same story, each depending on the character's reactions. Here is the version without reactions.

Billy went for a walk through the park on a Sunday morning. When he got to the playground, he sat down on a bench and read his book. Billy was distracted from his reading by the sounds of two little children arguing in the sandbox.

Give Billy some thoughts, feelings, and reactions.

Version 1

_____
_____
_____
_____
_____
_____
_____
_____

Version 2

_____
_____
_____
_____
_____
_____
_____
_____
_____

Chain–Reaction Maps

Stories are about characters. Events in stories cannot happen unless there are characters to act in the events or react to them. There are many, many different reactions that characters can have to events. For example, an event can be something as simple as a rain shower, and the reaction to this event might be simply that the character opens her umbrella. Or she might splash in puddles on the sidewalk.

A chain reaction is an event that causes a reaction in a character, which then makes another event happen, which causes yet another reaction, and so on. If you look at many of the stories you have read, you will see events causing reactions and those reactions causing further events.

Look at the chain reaction of events below.

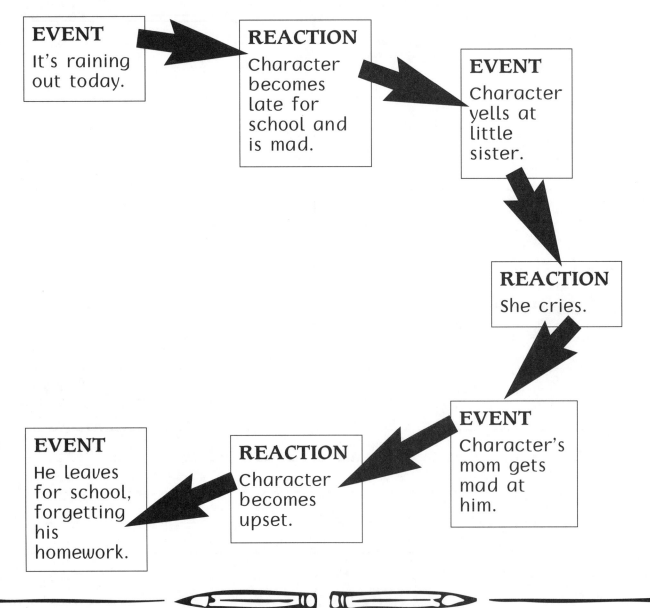

EVENT
It's raining out today.

REACTION
Character becomes late for school and is mad.

EVENT
Character yells at little sister.

REACTION
She cries.

EVENT
Character's mom gets mad at him.

REACTION
Character becomes upset.

EVENT
He leaves for school, forgetting his homework.

Chain-Reaction Maps

Try creating a chain-reaction outline. Start with one of the events in the box. Think of a character's reaction to the event and then keep building.

- The team wins the big game.
- A character finishes second in the race.
- A character loses her jacket.
- Someone's dog breaks free from its leash.

EVENT

REACTION

EVENT

REACTION

EVENT

REACTION

Showing vs. Telling
(What Good Writers Do!)

Many writers believe they must use lots of words to tell their readers what is happening in a story. However, good writers show rather than tell the events of a story. They let readers see people and ideas in action instead of simply describing what happens. So don't tell it in a story, show it. Don't say the old lady screamed. Bring her on and let her scream!

Look at the examples below and see how the writer changed the sentence from telling to showing.

"The big, shiny, red, round, apple in my lunch bag was really juicy."

Of course an apple is red, round, and shiny! Don't tell it, show it!

"When I sank my teeth into the ripe apple, its juice hit me square in the eye."

"Ron was really scared and frightened when he saw the skeleton start to walk."

Of course Ron would be scared! Don't tell it, show it!

"Ron's eyes bulged from his head and sweat dripped down his forehead as the skeleton clattered toward him."

"The little girl was very happy when she got her new bike."

Of course the girl would be happy! Don't tell it, show it!

"The biggest grin appeared on the little girl's face, and she jumped for joy when she saw her new bike."

Showing vs. Telling (Part 2)

Can you change these sentences so they show instead of tell the reader what is happening?

The people at the table thought the food was delicious.

_____

The broken car sat along the side of the road.

_____

The day was very hot.

_____

The trip to the amusement park was fun.

_____

The dog was mean.

_____

The classroom was a mess.

_____

The movie was awesome!

_____

Michael was very nervous before the math test.

_____

The house on the corner was very old.

_____

The mall was crowded and busy.

_____

Make Scenes More Vivid

All of the events in a story need to be described in detail that will make a clear picture in the reader's mind. Look at the following lines from first drafts. Then examine how they have been revised in second drafts.

DRAFT ONE

Sally and Jane went to the store.

Add details to make a clearer picture of the store.

DRAFT TWO

Sally and Jane headed downtown to the city's biggest mall. Right away, they took the glass elevator up to the second floor of the huge steel and glass building. All the clothing stores were on the second floor.

DRAFT ONE

Once upon a time there was a king.

Add details to make a clearer picture of the time.

DRAFT TWO

A long time ago, in a faraway land where unicorns still roamed and the fields were filled with wildflowers, there lived a king.

DRAFT ONE

The Smith family sat at the table ready to eat supper.

Add details to make a clearer picture of the Smith's dinner.

DRAFT TWO

The Smith family sat down at the big oak table that was filled with plates and plates of food. There were loaves of freshly baked bread, mashed potatoes, crisp fresh green beans, and a golden brown turkey. Delicious smells rose from all over the table.

Make Scenes More Vivid (Part 2)

Now that you have seen how adding details creates a clearer picture, revise the following sentences by adding more details.

DRAFT ONE

Frank and his friends decided to play in the park because it was such a nice day.

Add details describing what kind of day it was.

_____

_____

_____

_____

DRAFT ONE

Lisa knew right away she wanted the puppy in the store window. He was so cute.

Add details describing how cute the puppy was.

_____

_____

_____

_____

DRAFT ONE

George received a bike for his birthday. It was exactly the kind he wanted.

Add details describing the kind of bike George received.

_____

_____

_____

_____

Name _____

Simile Characters

Ted looked across the room at Jim, the new boy in school. People said that he was quick as lightning. Ted wondered if this was true. One thing Ted could see for sure, Jim was a muscular kid, as solid as a rock. Just then Annabel and Brenda walked over to Ted.

"Did you see that new guy?" asked Annabel. "He is so cute. His eyes are as blue as the deep, deep ocean, and his golden hair is as bright as the sun."

Brenda sighed, "Yes, and his lips are like red cherries. I also hear he's as brave as a knight in shining armor."

Ted groaned to himself.

In the story above, the characters use similes to describe Jim. Similes are figures of speech in which two things are compared using *like* or *as*. For example: She ran as fast as the wind, or his lips are like red cherries. Writers can use similes to describe a character's physical appearance, personality, and actions. The character of Jim would look something like the illustration above.

Can you create a simile character of your own? For each section below, list at least three words that would describe your character. Then think of any animals, objects, or events you can compare that trait to. If your character is tall, is he as tall as a redwood tree? If your character is loud, is she as loud as a bullhorn? Craft your similes using descriptive words and the objects you've listed below. Then draw a picture of your character using similes within the character's portrait. Label your portrait with the similes and give your character a name.

Physical Features	Simile
_____	_____
_____	_____
_____	_____
Personality	**Simile**
_____	_____
_____	_____
_____	_____
Actions	**Simile**
_____	_____
_____	_____
_____	_____

Endings: Put a Finishing Touch on Your Story

After hooking your readers with a fascinating lead and writing a captivating story, you need a finish that satisfies them. The last lines of a story are very important. They can leave a lasting impression of the whole story with the reader.

Some authors like to finish off their stories with a question that lingers in the reader's mind. Other authors like to leave a decision for their readers to make. The readers know the whole story but are left to decide how everything turns out at the end. Authors also use their last lines to wrap up their ideas, explaining how everything turns out. Whatever ending you choose, remember to take the time to come up with ideas that make an impact on your reader.

Here are some endings from published stories. Look carefully at what kind of ending the author used.

"All they wanted to do was to have peace to enjoy this strange, wild, blissful music from the great singer in space."

—from *Iron Giant* by Ted Hughes

"There they continued arguing to their hearts' content. After all the world would be a dull place indeed if we all agreed about absolutely everything wouldn't it?"

—from *Mick and Mack* by Terry Jones

"As Louis relaxed and prepared for sleep, all his thoughts were of how lucky he was to inhabit such a beautiful earth, how lucky he had been to solve his problems with music, and how pleasant it was to look forward to another night of sleep and another day tomorrow, and the fresh morning and the light that returns with the day."

—from *The Trumpet of the Swan* by E.B. White

"And Grannie Island never frowned at Granma Mainland's fancy ways ever again. I wonder why?"

—from *Katie Morag and the Two Grandmothers* by Mairi Hedderwick

"The child was smiling and in his hand he held the golden ball."

—from *The Clown of God* by Tomie DePaola

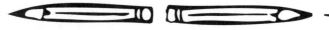

Part Four

Getting Ready to Publish

As students finish a writing project, there are a few steps for them to take to make their final product as good as it can be. The lessons in this section focus on making final corrections and revisions to their stories.

Mini-Lesson **21** Conferencing Tips

Conferencing with other student writers can be one of the most challenging parts of the writing process. I developed this lesson (pages 69–70) to help students learn how to identify problems in a piece of writing and practice giving other writers advice. I begin by reviewing the first selection on the reproducible with the class. Then we read the second sample together and discuss what advice we would give to the writer. Students can read and comment on the remaining samples independently. Once students are finished, we discuss all of the samples together.

Mini-Lesson **22** Decide Your Writing Is Set!

Not every piece of writing a student creates needs to be published. To help students decide which pieces they should publish, I like to do a lesson on figuring out when a story is set. The reproducible Decide Your Writing Is Set! (page 71) focuses on this stage of the writing process.

Mini-Lesson **23** My Story Checklist

Students can assess the final draft of their writing using this checklist (page 72). It gives students an opportunity to check grammar, structure, and style as well as evaluate their own understanding of the elements of good writing.

To help students keep track of all the things they need to check as they edit their stories for the last time, I have them used colored pencils to mark different types of errors. I review this procedure with students and then hand out copies of Final Edit (page 73). Students keep this page on hand whenever they are editing a story.

Mini-Lesson **24** Book Titles

One of the last stages in getting ready to publish a story is picking a title. In this lesson (page 74), students explore how titles help grab readers' attention.

Mini-Lesson **25** The Last Step: Publishing Students' Work

This part of the writing process can be time consuming. While there is value in letting students decide themselves in what form they'll publish, there are practicalities that need to be dealt with. The necessary supplies need to be available, and students must have the time to complete what becomes an art activity.

In addition, students need to be exposed to the variety of publishing formats and art techniques. Students can adapt the techniques you model to work with their own projects. Students are keen observers and quickly realize that even though the medium is the same, they can use it to stamp their work with their own personalities. Some of the different formats in which my students have published are: books, posters, scrolls, dioramas, articles, and more.

I do not introduce publishing formats at the same time as story structure; they are two different issues. Usually I wait until some students are halfway through a rough draft before we sit down for a mini-lesson on presentation. This may happen two or three days after the initial modeling presentation or more than a week later.

Managing the Publishing Process

Publishing is exciting. After all the writing, revising, and editing, the author begins to envision a final product. It is time to celebrate being a community of writers. However, publishing is also challenging if students get bogged down in some of the little details. Here are some tips that may help you and your students avoid the publishing woes.

✔ **Gathering Materials**

As we get closer to the publishing stage, I tell my students to start bringing in light cardboard materials, such as cereal boxes. I keep a container as the donation drop-off spot.

✔ **Creating Books**

When students are ready, I demonstrate the book-making process. Students can follow the directions on the reproducible (page 75). Creating the books is a motivating activity for students.

✔ **Comments Page**

I have students leave a blank page with the title Comments at the back of their books. I explain to students that they can ask readers to write comments about the book. As a class, we discuss how these comments are meant to be words of encouragement to fellow authors. This helps build an atmosphere of generosity in our community of writers.

✔ Using Computers for Writing

If you are fortunate enough to have a computer in the classroom, allow students to type their stories on the computer. I usually announce ahead of time when a period in the lab will be devoted to keyboarding. This way students have a piece of work ready to type or are ready to assist someone else in typing up a story.

✔ Volunteers

At first I felt that a student had to always be involved firsthand in the mechanics of publishing. However, in the real publishing world rarely does an author do this. So, with this in mind, I have no qualms about occasionally getting volunteers to help type stories.

✔ Artwork

Creating artwork can be very time-consuming. Most students start out eagerly creating a picture book with a picture on every page. Soon they get tired of drawing, and the quality declines. To help, I show students alternatives to the picture-book format. I show them books that have pictures and text on alternating pages. I also show them young-reader chapter books that have illustrations on every third or fourth page. Encourage students to vary their publishing forms with each piece of work.

Since in the publishing world writers don't do their own illustrations, I occasionally let students ask a classmate to create illustrations. I have them start with only illustrating covers. There are a few stipulations that I do enforce. Negotiations over illustrating cannot include money or completing someone else's assignments for them. One person may do artwork for another only if it does not take the artist away from his or her own work.

Conferencing Tips

When you are conferencing with someone you need to remember that the writer has selected you as someone who can help him or her with a piece of writing. While writers want to hear about the positive features of their writing, they also want to hear your ideas about how they can improve their writing.

Read the writing sample below and the advice the reader has given to the writer.

Michael got up at seven o'clock, and he go out of bed. He got dressed. He brushed his teeth. He washed his face. He combed his hair. He made his bed. He went downstairs. He had breakfast. He had cereal. He got his coat. He went outside he went to school.

You have a lot of information in the paragraph, but the sentences seem too short. It almost sounds like a list. Maybe you can combine some sentences together. Also, read all your words carefully. In the first line, it should be *got* instead of the word *go*.

What advice can you give to this writer?

_____

_____

_____

_____

_____

Conferencing Tips (Part 2)

Read the following paragraphs. What advice would you give to the writer of each of these paragraphs?

Jenny and Janice were best friends and they always did things together and they lived close by each other and they would do everything together. And the two friends were in the same class together and they liked the same things and they even looked the same.

What advice can you give this writer? _____

_____

_____

The boy and the dog were walking together and he saw something strange. His dog was brown and furry all over. He didn't know what the thing was. He went to look at it. Sally said hi, can I help? The building was dark he didn't know what it was. Scruffy was running.

What advice can you give this writer? _____

_____

_____

The family always ate together. They cooked all kinds of foods and they ate it. They ate a big turkey for supper today. When they ate the kids did the dishes after they ate. They ate in the dining room. When they ate they had guests over to eat.

What advice can you give this writer? _____

_____

_____

George and Fred found the last clue to the mystery. Do you think we got it? Yeah Do you think we got everything? No. Why? Look at the missing piece it doesn't fit. You're right, boy you're smart. Thanks. But you would have seen the mistake too. Do you think so? Yeah you are smart.

What advice can you give this writer? _____

_____

_____

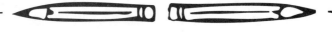

Decide Your Writing Is Set

A writer could keep on working at the same piece of writing for years and still not feel it was perfect. But a time comes when a writer just has to decide if a piece is as good as it can get. After you have written a draft, thought about it, conferenced with another student, and revised the draft, you need to make a major decision. Should you get the piece ready for others to read? If you decide yes, continue on the publishing path.

If, however you do not feel comfortable with it, you have two choices. You can take the work back and revise it more, or you can put the piece away for a later time and start with a fresh idea.

Remember, not everything a writer writes is meant for other readers' eyes. Other pieces just need to be shared. One fun part of being a writer is getting to make these decisions.

Here are some questions you should ask yourself when it comes time to make such a decision. Look at your writing and ask:

- Was I able to get my message across clearly?

- Will other people be interested in reading this?

- Will it make sense to others?

If you can answer yes to these questions, you may have a piece of writing that is begging to be published.

My Story Checklist

Have you finished writing your story?
Use this checklist to make sure you
have included all the elements you need
in your story.

	Yes	No
Have I written carefully and correctly?		
Have I used capital letters and punctuation marks correctly?		
Have I checked spelling?		
Is my handwriting clear and easy to read?		
Does my story make sense?		
Do I have a good beginning, middle, and end?		
Are my sentences in correct order?		
Are all my sentences about the topic?		
Are all my sentences complete?		
Did I write my story in an interesting way?		
Did I use the best words to tell my story?		
Did I provide enough detail in my story?		
Did I include details that are not needed?		
Did I show how the characters feel?		

Final Edit

When you feel your story is complete—that the plot, setting, and characters are set—it is time for a final edit. At this stage, you focus on things like spelling, punctuation, and word choice.

These things are very important because it is easier for a person to read a story if all of these elements are correct. Here are some steps for editing a story. You will need to use three different colored pens or pencils. Read through the whole story slowly, sentence by sentence and word by word. As you do this, use your colored pencils to do the following:

- Circle all words you think may be misspelled; circle with one colored pencil.

- Underline all words you think need to be changed with another color. You may need to change a word if you feel it is overused, it does not fit the sentence it's in, or you have discovered a better choice.

- Check all of the punctuation. Use your third colored pencil to add in, take out, or replace punctuation. This includes periods, commas, question marks, exclamation points, capital letters, and quotation marks.

- Cross out any words that are repeated or that you feel are unnecessary.

When you are done, your story will look like a mess of colors. Don't worry; this means you have edited your story very carefully. Now go back and use a dictionary to check the spelling of words you are unsure of, use a thesaurus to change words, and ask advice from fellow writers about punctuation.

Titles: How to Grab Your Reader Right Away!

You've spent a lot of time writing, revising, and editing your story and now you need a title to turn your story into a book. How can you find a title that will attract readers? Here are some ideas to help you create a catchy title.

✔ **Try a Summary Title:** As a newspaper headline does, a summary title explains what the story is all about. For example, *Boy Saves Town* is a title that tells you basically what happens in the story, although to learn who the boy is, why the town is in danger, and how the boy saves the town, we have to read the story.

✔ **Try a Preview Title:** These titles introduce the subject but with less detail than a summary title. An example is *The Flooding of Greensville*. We learn Greensville floods, but what else happens? Is the town destroyed?

✔ **Try a Teasing Title:** A teasing title doesn't reveal much about the plot but catches readers' attention with intriguing or dramatic words and phrases. What happens in a story called *Sunk*?

✔ **Try a Character Title:** This title uses a character's name, often that of the main character, for the title. Maybe an alternate title for *Boy Saves Town* could be *Fearless Fred*.

✔ **Try a Line Title:** A line title uses a phrase or quotation from the story, often one that is repeated or has a special meaning, as the title of the story. Such a title for our example story might be *Better Get Your Swimsuit On*.

✔ **Try a Question Title:** This title uses a question that someone from the story may have asked. *Boy Saves Town* might also be called *How Can I Rescue Someone if I Can't Swim?*

Take a look at some of the interesting book titles that can be found in your library. Here are just a few you might come across. Can you identify what type of title the author has used?

- Say Cheese
- I'd Rather Be Eaten by Sharks!
- Harriet the Spy
- Freaky Friday
- Out of the Dust

- Beware the Fish!
- Who's Got Gertie and How Can We Get Her Back?
- It's Like This Cat
- The Great Gilly Hopkins
- The Secret Garden

Book Making

1. Take two pieces of cardboard (of similar thickness) and cut them into the size you want for your book.

2. Leaving a small space between the two pieces of cardboard, tape them together.

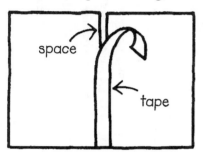

space   tape

3. Try folding your book to see if it closes properly. If it does, use a large sheet of paper to create the cover. You can use any kind of paper, including wrapping paper, construction paper, and contact paper.

4. Place the sheet under the book cover. Make sure the sheet is larger than the book. (Leave approximately $1\frac{1}{2}$ inch on each side.) Carefully cut from the corners of the sheet to the corners of the cardboard.

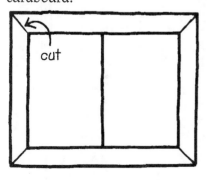

cut

5. Fold the top and bottom over and then glue or tape down the fold. Tuck the corners in. Then glue or tape down the corners. Then fold and tape down the two other sides.

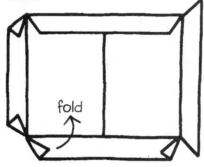

fold

6. Once your cover is on, fold the book closed.

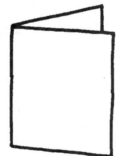

7. Now get the pages for your book ready. Once you know how many pages your book will be, count out the necessary sheets of paper and fold them together in half. (One sheet is four pages of a book, using both sides.) Include sheets for a Dedication Page, an About-the-Author Page, and a Comments Page. Attach one extra page as a glue-down page. Staple the

sheets in the center using a long-arm stapler.

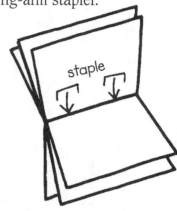

staple

8. Place the sheets inside the cover. Run tape or glue along the edges of the glue-down page, attaching it to both halves of the book cover.

glue or tape

9. Glue a white page to the front for a cover illustration.

Answer Keys for Proofreader's Challenge

Proofreader's Challenge
Walking Down Fig Street

Have you been very afraid of something, only to find out later that it wasn't scary at all? Well, let me tell you about a time I did just that.

In september I started at a new school. Soon i found the shortest way to get my new school. I would walk across a empty field, down a back lane, and turn on to a tiny little street called fig street and that would take me to the school parking lot. i liked going this way 'cause it seemed that no other kids walked this way to school. It gave me a chance to be by myself and instead of walking with a large group of kids.

After the first few weeks I notice that I wad't walking my favorite path alone. Each morning, as I came out of the back lane and turned onto Fig Street, I heard footsteps behind me. The first time I didn't think much of it and as I got to the end of the street the footsteps disappeared. Now you may wonder why I didn't just turn around and look. The truth was that I was to scared to.

Everyday after I turn on Fig street I would hear the foot steps behind me. Each day I became a little braver and I would turn my head slily and look over my shulder. At first all I saw was a long shadow. The next time I turned my head, I could see a figure was dressed in black.

Little by little, I saw more of the figure. It appeared to have a black hood and long black robe. The footsteps moved so slowly they made me nervous.

Finally I couldn't take it none more. I decided the next day I would face the figure.

The next morning, as i turned on to fig Street, I heard the footsteps again. This time the footsteps slowed down, as if the figure was ready to pounce. And so I turned around and screed at the figure, "STOP FOLLOWING ME!"

Imagine my horror and embarrassment, as I found myself facing an elderly nun who was out for her daily walk.

Proofreader's Challenge
The Statue

once upon a time, in a land far, far away they're lived a king king clement's wife had died many years ago and left him with one daughter. Princess Elizabeth was the most precious thing to king Clement whatever his daughter wanted king clement would give her. one day the King announced that a new statue would be shown at the courtyard fountain on the opening day of the county fair. soon all the townspeple were talking about the statue to be place in the courtyard stories were spreading that was the king's daughter, princess Elizabeth herself who had made it.

while all this talk was going on peter the Baker was out of town and did not her the stories on the day of the fair, everybody gathered in the castle courtyard music was playing, games were set up and food served halfway through the celebration trumpets sounded as the king unveiled the statue for the town's fountain.

When the statue was uncovered the crowd oohed and ahed and clapped and cheered "beautiful" yelled a group of woman "its superb" called the men at the back now the strange thing about this all was that the statue was quite ugly of course since everybody knew who made it, but nobody dared say anything bad in fear of the king's anger. All but poor Peter the baker who did not know this. he laughed out loud and exclaimed, "We can't put that thing in the courtyard its embarrassing,

the whole crowd went silent and they turned to the king standing on the steps of the castle, everybody waited to hear the order for Peter to be thrown in the dungen the king spoke slowly, "come here, young man," Peter went to stand next to the king my loyal subject, said the king, my daughter and I have played a little trick we wished to see if people would be honest with us, we brought out this hideous statue and had everybody believe my daughter made it, but he is her real one, the guards brought out a statue that was remarkable, this young man, said the King, was the only person who was honest with us, he shown me he can be trusted in fact trusted enough to have my daughter's hand in marriage, after that, peter was not known as Peter the baker anymore.

Proofreader's Challenge
Mr. Singular

mr. Singular was a man of habit. He liked things to be same each and every day.

This way he knew what to expected. He ate his supper at the same time each day, visit ed his mother each Sunday, and clean his house on fridays after the work week ended.

One of Mr. Singular's favorite habits was to walk to work. Each day he wake up a little earlier than necessary so he could walk thru the park on his way to work. halfway through he would stop at the same park bench sit and read his morning paper, and eat his muffin.

Now the other important thing to know about Mr. Singular was that he was a very lonely man. You see, other than his mother, Mr. singular had know other family or friends he could visit. You mite be wondering why this was so, but the simpli fact was that Mr. Singular just didn't feel comfortable around people. He tried joining a stamp club but felt akward around all them others, who knew so much more than him. he tried writing pen pal letters but didn know what to say. So finaly Mr. Singular gave up trying and instead just wished for a friend.

His daily path to work reminded him how lonely was he. He pass the small pond and wished he had someone to go fishing with, he walked by the baseball feld and wished he had some to play ball with, he passed the man who fed the birds each day and wished he had a friend to share things with, and he saw people chatting at the bus stop and wished he had someone to talk to.

Proofreader's Challenge
Mr. Singular (part 2)

One day, Mr. Singular noticed something different about his usual moning walk.

The man who feeded the birds was not at his usual spot.

how strange, thought Mr. Singular. He is here every day giving bread crums to the birds. What could have happened to him!

Just then the bird feeding man slowly walked up the path with his hands in his pockets. He plopped down on the bench next to Mr. Singular and sighed. the man looked so disturbed that Mr. Singular did not even think about being uncomfortable when he asked, is something the matter?"

"oh, yes," the man replied. You see each day I save bread crumbs to bring the birds. But somehow this morning all my cupboards were bare. I didn't half a single scrap, and it is to early for the stores to be open. My poor feathered friends will have to go with out for the first time today.

Mr. Singular looked down at his muffin. "Here, use this, I'm sure the birds will love it," "But this is your breakfast," said the man. "That's okay," said mr. Singular. The next day when Mr. Singular sat on his usual bench, the man appeared again, this time with bread crums and two muffins.

The two men meet each morning to feed the birds. Soon after there first conversation, the bird man suggested they meet at the pond in the park on saturday and go fishing. The following weekend they met at the park to play ball.

Sometimes what we wish for is staring at us all we need to do is notice it.

Proofreader's Challenge
The Revenge of Johnny Cupcake

Every school has a child that is considered the school bully. There is that one student that terrorizes every body. At Franklin elementary School that bully was Meatbone Malone. Meatbone received this name for all his reputation for chewing on huge meatbones in the lunchroom. rumors flew that some of these meatbones were former students. Of course everybody knew this was false but it added to the legend of meatbone malone.

They're were many storys about meatbone Malone that were told to new students, including the day he tied a boys shoelaces to the flagpole with the boy still wearing the shoes and the time he stole a pair of glasses from a girl. But the famousest tale was about the day Meatbone Malone met up with Little Johnny Cupcake.

Now this was not Johnny's real name. But once in the lunchroom Meatbone seen Johnny with a cupcake, and squished the cupcake in his face, and decided that Little Johnny Cupcake was johnny's new nickname. Johnny was small boy, with big thick glasses, red hair, and many freckles. Johnny always had his nose in a book he was just the kind of student Meatbone loved to pick on.

One day Johnny was walking to his class, reading a book wile he walk. he was preoccupied because his African violet flowers were wilting and Johnny was searching for a solution to his dilema. As he read through his book someone banged into him. Wham! his glasses and book fell to the floor. Of course Johnny being already upset about his flowers did not stop to think, and blurted out "Watch where your going you clumsy ox."

When Johnny put on his glasses, he could see two huge feet next to him. He looked way up to see the dastardly smile of Meatbone Malone. A hushed fell in the hall.

Proofreader's Challenge
The Revenge of Johnny Cupcake (part 2)

Everyone knew this was the end for Johnny Cupcake. No one dared talk back to Meatbone, not ever.

Johnny jump to his feet and started running. He knew his only chance was escape.

Meatbone thundered a long behind.

Johnny turned the corner and reached a dead end the only thing to do was duck into the boys bathroom. Johnny baked against the wall and trembled. BOOM BOOM the foot steps approched and the pane of glass on the door rattled. The bathroom door flew open and then stood hugo shadowy bulk of Meatbone Malone.

Johnny pressed himself against the mirrors on the back wall of the bathroom as meatbone stepped closer and closer. Just as Johnny could feel the hot air blowing out of Meatbone's nostrals, the bully stopped, looked up into the mirror and froze. he started backing up further and further and then raced out of the bathroom.

What Meatbone had seen in the mirror that day so the story goes was his own reflection surrounded by fiery flames. In fact it was such a hideous site that Meatbone transfered schools later that day. That's how terrified he was.

The part of the legend that has never been told and only known to johnny was that he was thankful he just finished reading about reflections in his encyclopedia. Little johnny used his flame red marble to reflect against the bathroom taps and onto the bathroom mirror.

Sometimes brains can beat brawn.

Proofreader's Challenge
Buddy and Sweetie

The best summer I'd ever had was the year I met Buddy and sweetie. i was eleven years old that summer, and I'll never forget it.

It did not start out in such a positively way. Just before the end of school year, my dad got a announcement from his job saying that we would have to move to australia to open a new office for his company. my dad sold insurance, whatever that is.

one night at dinner Mama and daddy discussed our family's plans. At the beginning of school vacation Mama and Daddy would fly to australia. Daddy would set up his new office while Mama would search for a new house for us. i will be going to spend the summer with Grandpa and Grandma.

I was very sad about this news. I loved my grandpa and Grandma but they lived on a farm far away from any other kids. They're would be no one to play with. what does a eleven-year-old girl have in common with a seventy-year-old couple, i thought.

But there was no use morning about it. plans were set. I would be on the farm all summer until Mama returned to pick me up. the day Mama dropped me off at my Granparents' farm was a very uncomfortable day. I was very polite to them, but they seemed like strangers. Since they lived so far away, I never spent much time with them. I felt very gloomy watching my mother drive away, leaving me with these two ancient people.

Proofreader's Challenge
Buddy and Sweetie (Part 2)

That first night Grandma and Grandpa tried to help me get used to the place. Grandma made a supper that I must admit smelled delicious. Grandpa kept on trying to tell jokes but couldn't remember the endings. I couldn't help but laugh, but I was still sad.

I had been in bed what seemed like only a short time when I felt a nudge on my shoulder. It was Grandpa with a flashlight in his hand, all dressed. He told me to get my clothes and follow him to the barn. It was four o'clock in the morning.

Once inside the barn, Grandpa tooked me to two pens where horses stretched out on hay. A man who I later found out was an animal doctor was there. Grandpa informed me that the horses were ready to give birth and if i wanted, the babies could be mine. I was amazed.

When the sun came up that morning, I was the owner for a male and a female horse. I named them Buddy and Sweetie. For the rest of the summer, i spent my days with Buddy and Sweetie. A day usually went as follows: feed the horses, take them for they're morning walk, groom them, feed them again, walk them again, and then let them rest with their mothers.

by the end of the summer, i was totally attached to the horses and to my grandparents as well. I made a promise that each summer vacation I would return to see my grandparents and my horses.

Name _____

Proofreader's Challenge
Digger's Mistake

Once upon a time, there were two dogs that lived by side by side as neighbors. For many years the two dogs spend much time together playing ball, going for walks, and barking at cats. Other dogs considered the two good friends.

Now max was the bigger of them two dogs and greatly admired by others who said he could have been a show dog. Digger was smaller, and a runt of a dog and could never do things quit as well as Max. he could not run as fast or bark as loud. Max knew which postman to bark at and how to stay away from the dogcatchers. Digger admired max and would do anything for his friend.

One day Max received a new blanket from his masters. He put it in his doghouse and went for a stroll in the afternoon when he returned he found digger in his dog house sleeping on the new blanket. Now it was not that Digger meant to take something from his friend; he just wanted to share something that belonged to his dear friend; He knew he should have have asked but sometimes dogs make mistakes.

Digger apologized over and over to his friend but Max said told him him to leave. For days Digger never seen his friend. He no longer had anyone to play ball, to chase cats, with or to bark with. A few more days pass and then Max stopped by wondering if digger wanted to go to the park.

Of course digger said yes he missed his friend so much Max said he had missed Digger to.

digger was relieved that Max finally understand that sometimes mistakes happen.

37

Notes

80